SECRETS OF THE KINGDOM

D0085235

SECRETS OF THE K

SECRETS OF THE KINGDOM

*British Radicals from the Popish Plot to the
Revolution of 1688–1689*

Richard L. Greaves

Stanford University Press • *Stanford, California* • *1992*

Stanford University Press
Stanford, California
© 1992 by the Board of Trustees of the
Leland Stanford Junior University
Printed in the United States of America
CIP data are at the end of the book

Published with the assistance of
The Florida State University

To
Ted and Judith Underwood,
and to
Christopher Hill,
Doyen of Stuart Historians

Preface

This volume completes a trilogy, the first two volumes of which were *Deliver Us from Evil: The Radical Underground in Britain, 1660–1663* (New York: Oxford University Press, 1986) and *Enemies Under His Feet: Radicals and Nonconformists in Britain, 1664–1677* (Stanford, Calif.: Stanford University Press, 1990). The trilogy covers dissident activities in England, Scotland, Ireland, and British exile communities on the Continent from the restoration of the monarchy in 1660 to the revolution of 1688–89. The first volume explores radical undertakings from the uprisings of John Lambert and John Venner to the northern rebellion in 1663; the second encompasses militant activity from the Second Dutch War to the period following Charles' proclamation of an indulgence in 1672; and the third extends from the Popish Plot to the "Glorious Revolution," with special attention to the Bothwell Bridge insurrection, the so-called Rye House conspiracies, the Argyll and Monmouth rebellions, and radical involvement in the revolution of 1688–89. The trilogy thus underscores both the continuity and the geographical range of radical activity in all three kingdoms from the restoration to the revolution—or perhaps more accurately, from revolution to revolution.

I use the anachronistic term "radical" to refer to the more extreme forms of dissent, both political and religious. Radicals endorsed active disobedience to laws they found offensive. This disobedience took such forms as physical resistance to authorities, the publication of illegal works, acts of rebellion, and even assassination. Some radicals were republicans, but as Gary De Krey has remarked, "the true measures of radicalism are not to be found in republican institutional blueprints but rather in advocacy of a wide and free electorate, accountable government, and individual rights secured through appropriate actions, including resistance."[1] Many radicals were nonconformists, although some were members of the established church while others had no significant religious interests. Not all nonconformists were radicals, however, nor is the term "radical" synonymous with particular dissenting groups, such as General Baptists or Congregationalists (Independents). On the contrary, radicals were to be found among all Protestant groups in late Stuart Britain.

I would add two further caveats. First, we must understand Stuart radicals in their own context, not that of modern radicalism. Although Stuart radicals did not espouse a common vision of the society to which they aspired, they were united in their dislike of arbitrary government, Roman Catholicism, prelacy, and the persecution of Protestants. This was their frame of reference, and we must understand them in these terms rather than employing anachronisms. Second, in analyzing the nature and significance of radical activity in late Stuart Britain I am neither suggesting that I approve of its tenets nor contending, as did Whig historians, that they were destined to triumph. On the contrary, while some have found favor with later ages, others have been repudiated or discarded as obsolete. Historiographically, this trilogy will, I hope, contribute to the emerging re-evaluation of late Stuart Britain undertaken by such scholars as Lois Schwoerer, Richard Ashcraft, Gary De Krey, Jonathan Barry, William Speck, and Janelle Greenberg.

Much of this volume deals with the controversial conspiracies collectively (and misleadingly) known as the Rye House Plot. Whether these conspiracies actually existed has been disputed since the 1680s. More recently, such historians as Maurice Ashley and Tim Harris have essentially discounted the existence of the plotting because of the nature of the evidence; in Harris' judgment, "there is no evidence to suggest that such groups ever did contemplate such a rebellion," and Ashley calls the Rye House assassination plot "one of the great historical myths."[2] Other scholars, such as Ashcraft, De Krey, and Barry, believe the conspiracy was real. Indeed, the Argyll and Monmouth rebellions in 1685 can be seen as an outgrowth of the Rye House plotting, as Robin Clifton and Peter Earle suggest.

The problem of evaluating the evidence is complicated by the origins of the conspiracy in the context of the Popish Plot, when both Whigs and Tories freely engaged in subornation, severely undermining the integrity of the judicial system. John Kenyon's landmark study *The Popish Plot* does not fully reveal the extent of the abuse of the court system by men motivated by political gain and self-preservation. The sorry specter of subornation, played out against a background of two decades of radical agitation and domestic espionage, must make any historian extremely wary in assessing the Rye House evidence.

The nature of this evidence is varied. Fifteen key figures who made substantive statements fall roughly into five categories. The first of these comprises four men, each of whom confessed freely in the early stages of discovery and testified for the prosecution against his former colleagues. Each is vulnerable to charges of self-serving as well as possible prevarication. This group includes Josiah Keeling, who turned informer and provided the government with its first substantial opportunity to crush the conspirators. A late recruit, Keeling knew little and had never been in contact with anyone of prominence. Much more valuable is the extensive testimony of Robert West, the staunchly Whig barrister of the Middle Temple. Although parts of his confession incorporate hearsay, the basic outline stands up very well when compared with the testimony of others; his contacts were limited to middle- and lower-level conspirators. More problematic is the evidence of Colonel John Rumsey, a Cromwellian veteran and customs collector at Bristol, whose recollection was sometimes garbled. The most enigmatic of this group was William Lord Howard of Escrick, who had a predilection for conspiracy: a member of the Leveller faction that had schemed to restore the monarchy in the 1650s, he was briefly imprisoned; after spying on the Netherlands in the Third Dutch War, he worked as an agent for William of Orange, twice going to the Tower for interrogation.[3] Although Howard embellished his story, its general framework withstands critical scrutiny.

The four men in the second category made relatively full confessions after they were captured. Two of them—Ford Lord Grey, an outspoken Whig, and Nathaniel Wade, a Bristol attorney—were ap-

prehended in the Monmouth rebellion. Although Grey's statement
is self-serving, occasionally vague, and based at times on hearsay,
when the second-hand passages are discounted and allowance is
made for incidental factual errors, his account is reasonably sound.
Wade's testimony, refreshingly candid and largely devoid of self-
serving comments, frequently corroborates the statements of others.
Like Grey and Howard, he could testify about his personal involvement with such major figures as the earl of Shaftesbury, the duke of
Monmouth, and William Lord Russell. The third figure, William
Carstares, an intimate of the earl of Argyll and another of William of
Orange's intelligence operatives, confessed only under torture. The
last man in this category, James Holloway, a Bristol linen merchant,
provided a detailed account of his involvement in the schemes of
West and his associates.

The four men in the third category admitted a degree of com-
plicity in the plotting but said little about their activities. Three of
them were executed, two of them (Russell and Walcott) for their role
in the Rye House plotting. Russell not only confessed having been
present in a cabal that discussed an attack on the king's guards, but
also admitted, "I have heard many things & say'd some things contrary to my duty." Notes of the confession of Captain Thomas Walcott, a Shaftesbury intimate, are meager, but he admitted involvement in the conspiracy: Shaftesbury, he said, had enlisted him in "an
Vndertaking to Assert the peoples Just Libertyes, which were in haz-
ard," and he identified the commanders of the proposed rebellion as
Shaftesbury in London, Monmouth in Taunton and Bristol, Russell
in Devon, and Lord Brandon in Chesire. His testimony substantially
agrees with West's account.[4]

Monmouth, who is also in the third category and was executed,
had a personal meeting with Charles and James in November 1683 in
which he acknowledged "his guilt, & the share he had in the Conspiracy"; he also gave "an account of the whole conspiracy, naming
all those concerned in it, which were more then those [who] had
allready been mentioned by severall Witnesses." In December 1685,
the fourth man, John Hampden, who had previously been found
guilty of a misdemeanor—conspiracy to launch an insurrection—on
the basis of Howard's testimony, pleaded guilty to charges of high
treason when the state acquired, in Grey, a second witness.